Kia's Manatee

by Mary Vigliante Szydlowski
illustrated by Lori Kiplinger Pandy

Kia's Manatee

Written By Mary Vigliante Szydlowski
Illustrated by Lori Kiplinger Pandy

Text Copyright © 2011 Mary Vigliante Szydlowski
Book design and illustrations © 2011 Lori Kiplinger Pandy

Published by
Operation Outreach-USA Press
Holliston, MA

ISBN 978-0-9792144-5-5

Printed in the United States of America

To Frank,
With Love

Kia lived near a little bay. It wasn't like the ones she'd seen in books. They were pretty. They were clean. This little bay was not! The water was dirty green. Not blue.

Sometimes it was brown.

1

Nobody visited the little bay. Not boats. Not animals. Not people.

Just Kia.

The little bay was filled with trash. Lots and lots of trash. There were empty bottles and bags. Jugs of every size and color. There were paper cups and paper plates. And lots of old newspapers. They covered the banks. They floated on the water.

Even though it was dirty, Kia liked the little bay. It was quiet. It was a good place to think.

One day a strange thing happened.
Kia saw something in the water.
Something big! Something very big.

What *was* it?

It was very fat. It was gray. Was it a baby whale? Or a walrus? It had a big flat tail. Then its nose popped out of the water. Kia couldn't believe her eyes. It was a sea cow! A manatee!

"What are you doing here?" Kia asked. "This isn't a good place for you."

Kia waved her arms. She wanted to scare it away. But she stopped.

The manatee's back was cut and bleeding.
A boat must have hit it.

The manatee couldn't go back to the big
bay. There were too many boats there.
The manatee was hurt. It couldn't
swim fast. It couldn't get
out of their way.

The little bay was safe. There were no boats here. It was a good place for a hurt manatee. *If only it wasn't so dirty!*

Kia sat down on the bank. She didn't know what to do. Would the dirty water make the manatee sick? She didn't want the manatee to die!

Kia picked up a ball of fishing line. She found a bag under a bush. She put the line in the bag. Kia picked up an old tin can. Lots of paper cups. A red jug. And some bottles. She put them in the bag too.

Soon the bag was full. Kia had cleaned a few feet of the bank.

Kia was thinking. "If only I could get rid of all this trash. Then the manatee could stay here. It could get well!"

It was a big job. But Mama always said Kia could do anything! *When she set her mind to it.*

Kia ran home. She got a big box of trash bags. She took the rake. Then she found a long rope and some work gloves. She also took Mama's big blue basket.

Kia worked all morning. She picked up the trash along the bank.

Then tied the rope to Mama's basket. She threw the basket into the water. Kia pulled the rope. Trash floated into the basket.

There were lots of bags and bottles. Even an old shoe. Kia pulled the basket out of the water. She dumped everything into a bag. She raked under the bushes. Then she raked near the water.

The manatee watched Kia.

Mama wanted to know where Kia was getting all the trash.
Kia told her about the manatee.

"The work will go fast if we work together," said Mama.

They worked till supper.
The manatee watched them leave.

"Do you think it knows we're trying to help?" Kia asked.
"I think so," said Mama. "Let's tell old Mr. William about your manatee. He has a rowboat. He can get the trash in the deep water."

Daddy came home from work.
Kia told him about the manatee.

Mama made a lot of phone calls
that night.

So did Kia's father.

The next day lots of people came to their house. They wanted to help clean up the little bay. Daddy's friends. Mama's friends. Aunt Taneka and Uncle Roy. Grandma Lula and Aunt Bessie. Mr. William. His friend Mr. Louis. And his wife Miss Isabel. Everyone wanted to help Kia save the manatee.

They worked all day Saturday.

And after church on Sunday.

When they were done, the little bay looked beautiful! Every piece of trash was gone!

On Monday Kia went to the library. She wanted to learn more about manatees.

Kia checked the manatee every day. It was getting better.

Mr. William made a red and white sign.
He stuck it in the bank.

It said, **"GO SLOW! MANATEE!"**

Sometimes the manatee went into the big bay to feed.
But it always came right back.

Then one day the manatee was gone.

Kia was worried. Where was the manatee?

A few days later the manatee came back.
It brought a friend. The little bay would
make a good home for them. A clean,
quiet place to live and raise a family.

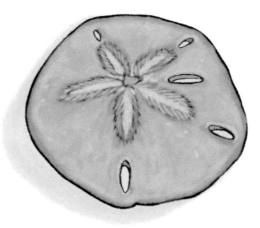